DALMATIAN SONNETS AND OTHER POEMS

BY PAULA VON PRERADOVIĆ

ENGLISH TRANSLATION

BY VICKO MARELIĆ AND IRINA PAVLOVIĆ

DALMATIAN SONNETS AND OTHER POEMS

BY PAULA VON PRERADOVIĆ

ENGLISH TRANSLATION

BY VICKO MARELIĆ AND IRINA PAVLOVIĆ

STUDIES IN CENTRAL EUROPEAN HISTORY,
CULTURE & LITERATURE

SERIES EDITED BY GÜNTER BISCHOF

UNIVERSITY OF NEW ORLEANS PRESS

Dalmatian Sonnets and Other Poems
By Paula von Preradović
Translated by Vicko Marelić and Irina Pavlović

Studies in Central European History, Culture and Literature Series
Edited by Günter Bischof

ISBN: 9781608012749

Cover and interior design by: Kevin Stone

The Map of Dalmatia in the Austrian Empire is used with permission from The State Archives in Zadar, Croatia.

Printed in the United States of America on FSC certified paper.

First edition.

University of New Orleans Press
2000 Lakeshore Drive
New Orleans, Lousiana 70148
unopress.org

CONTENTS

INTRODUCTION

PAULA VON PRERADOVIĆ
'POET BETWEEN PEOPLES.'

PAULA VON PRERADOVIĆ

(1887-1951)

PREFACE

It is with much elation that the Molden family, the descendants of Paula von Preradović and Ernst Molden, has learned of Vicko Marelić and Irina Pavlović's endeavor to translate some of Paula von Preradović's most beautiful poetry into English. No family member alive today has had the opportunity to know our grandmother, who died in 1951, partly of the late effects of Nazi torture. But in a certain way–through the many stories told by her sons Otto and Fritz, who were our fathers–she has always been present. A part of our universe, connecting us with a sphere that had long faded, and thus widening our own horizons through a strong emotional link to the past.

Hence it is striking to us that her earlier poems and prose must have had a similar effect on their readers when they were published in the 1920s, 1930s and 1940s. They often spoke of a world that, from the vantage point of post-imperial Vienna, was "lost": the Mediterranean coastlands of Croatia, Slovenia and Northeastern Italy, and above all the Dalmatian islands where Paula's ancestors had built a lineage of military men–officers of the Hapsburg navy–and poets.

The Dalmatian Sonnets were first published in Vienna in 1933, as Paula von Preradović's second volume of poems. Now, they are to become the first English translation of our grandmother's work, and anglophone readers will at long last have access to these lines, which contain and convey more than a particular moment in the history of Austrian literature. They also appear to transmit, like a delayed message from a long-defunct lyrical radio antenna, a condensed feeling from a bygone age of Austrian cultural and political history: the feeling of loss of the "old Austria's" larger world, a longing to something which's definitive departure could not yet be fully realized.

Our grandmother lived between, or rather: in, two worlds. One was the sun-drenched southern universe of her Dalmatian childhood and youth; the other the rather rough reality of a country that had abruptly shrunk to a small, politically shaken and divided republic on the northern slopes of the Alpes. As a poet and highly active intellectual, she found herself in the center of turmoil of Austria's First Republic, of the Austro-Fascist regime, and of Nazi rule. Her father-in-law, Berthold Molden, died a few weeks before being deported–like his younger brother Heinrich–to the death camps of the Holocaust, and Paula and her husband Ernst found themselves banned from their vocations under Nazi rule because of their Austrian patriotism. As their sons, our fathers, took up arms against the Nazis, it was like a loud and younger echo of her own resistance, and she would pay a high price for both.

The Dalmatian Sonnets were written before this suffering, but Paula and her family, as well as that of her husband Ernst Molden, had lost much in the First World War. Kin who had fallen in the war, of course, but also the wide, multicultural lands of the Hapsburg empire. If you come into Pula and Istria today and look for the house of Paula's youth, at the edge of a park with age-old trees from all corners of the world, if you wander through the olive groves, watch the sunset and breathe the aromatic air, if you listen to the groove of the cicadas, then you can comprehend the great longing that transcends from many of her poems, and especially those you find on these pages.

This part of her universe is captured in our grandmother's novel "Pave and Pero" that traces the dramatic live of her own grandparents. Its other side can be felt in the text of the national anthem, which she wrote after the Second World War for the reborn Austrian nation.

We hope that this book may serve as an introduction into this world of Paula von Preradović. We thank Vicko and Irina for their initiative and translations and Guenter Bischof, great scholar and sponsor of Austrian history and culture, for his generous support in bringing these translations to print.

Peter and Berthold Molden
Alpbach, Tyrol, in January 2024

INTRODUCTION

A NOTE ON THE PROJECT AND TRANSLATION

IRINA PAVLOVIĆ

Dear readers,

It is with great pleasure that we can present to you the first ever English translation of a selection of poetry by the little known but important Austrian poet Paula von Preradović. This translation, which includes poems from the collection *Südliche Sommer* and *Dalmatinische Sonneten*, came about thanks to the enthusiastic co-operation between two research fellows at Centre Austria in New Orleans between 2018-19. These works of poetry offer a unique insight into the landscape and soul of the eastern Adriatic, a former part of the Austrian Empire, where the poet spent part of her childhood.

During our one-year research program at the Austrian Marshall Plan Centre for European Studies at the University of New Orleans, me and Vicko Marelić chose to translate *viribus unitis* a selection of poetry by von Preradović. For us it was a special honour- a challenging combination of accurate linguistic and cultural co-ordination as well as a concern to as authentically as possible make accessible a selection of poetry of this great Austrian daughter to an English-speaking audience. While challenging and long lasting, the project has been an immensely rewarding voyage of discovery.

The present collection is by no means a professional undertaking. Vicko and I are not literary scholars. Rather we selected these poems through our joint feeling and acquaintance with the plethora of motifs in question, instead of calculation, which makes our translations equally personal and idiosyncratic. Like Paula, our identities are also perched between countries, which has given us a richness of expression that has found a fertile field in this work of translation.

Thanks to our three origins and working languages (German, Croatian and English) as well as our three different academic backgrounds (philology, history and linguistics) we worked with a special synergy. Vicko Marelić, a British-born historian and francophone studies graduate, comes from the southern Dalmatian Island of Korčula. Without his detailed knowledge of the maritime minutia and characteristics of the region's landscape, such a precise translation would not have been possible. As an English and Slavic studies graduate, I am partially like Paula von Preradović herself, an Austrian of Croatian and Serbian origin, a Yugoslav mixture *par excellence,* with a part of my family coming from the Dalmatian hinterland. Above all, I am a north Tyroler living in northern Germany.

I am still surprised that during my school and university education I learnt nothing about Paula von Preradović's literary *opus* as well as her courageous participation in the anti-Nazi resistance in Austria. Compared to her grandfather, Petar, a well-known Croatian Romanticist poet of the Illyrian movement who reached the high position of a general in the Austrian army, Paula's literary opus was comparatively unknown. All the more reason to thank Vicko Marelić for initiating this translation project which gave me an insight into her life and work.

The poems here are mostly taken from Paula's second volume of poems where she writes in sonnet form about one of her homelands, Dalmatia, which is also mine and Vicko's common homeland. The other half of my heart beats for Austria, for which I feel a special bond with Paula von Preradović.

The freedom we took in generally not following the sonnet form in translation came about thanks to the fact that we decided to communicate her linguistic heritage through focusing on her mystical vocabulary. Honoring the meter of her verse would have been too much at the expense of her unique expressiveness. We decided to modify her diction as little as possible in a translation to give a sense of what we felt she meant.

The result is raw yet flamboyant, just like the Karst hinterland and the lush greenery of Dalmatia. Her language is pietistic, conservative and thus revolutionary, being yet inviting in equal measure. It is this contradiction in Paula's poetic declaration of love and devotion to the unique beauties of one of her homelands that captures the reader's imagination. In the spirit of her beliefs that saw a connection between the permanent nature of the landscape and the divine, she succeeds in creating a remarkably workable trinity between mankind, the divine and the environment. With this translation, we wanted to pay tribute to this great daughter of Austria.

Irina Pavlović, 1. August 2023

DALMATIA, A HISTORICAL OVERVIEW

VICKO MARELIĆ

"*Landschaften wie Dalmatien, sind sie nicht das Wunderbarste in der Welt*"
Ernst Jünger, *Dalmatinischer Aufenthalt*, 1932

Paula von Preradović's childhood and youth between 1899-1901 and 1905-1913 was spent in Pula on the Adriatic, inspiring her her to pen lyrical poetry in praise of the Dalmatian coast where the Habsburgs had their maritime avenue to the world. Her yearning for the sea is a symbol for the unfulfilled wish to the land of her early youth, the *Altösterreich* homeland that sunk forever in 1918. The poetic opus of von Preradović 'became known early on as the poet of the Istrian and Dalmatian coastal landscapes and as mediator between cultures- with her first volume of poetry *Südliche Sommer* and *Dalmatinische Sonette*[1]' showing the unmistakable imprint of the sea that seems permanently moored into her poetry.

As an Austrian poet with roots in the Croatian part of the monarchy, her writing links these two worlds together through the universal medium of literature. Her rich literary opus often focuses on universal and eternal themes such as the beauty of the landscape, the mysteries of the divine and the power of the

1 Johann Georg Lughofer, *Bilder und Funktionen des Mittelmeeres bei Paula von Preradović,* in: Germanistica Euromediterrae: međunarodni časopis za euromediteransku germanistiku, Vol. 1, No. 1. 2019, 109.

infinite. Like the doyen of Mediterranean studies, Ferdinand Braudel, von Preradović is not Mediterranean born. Yet through a deep immersion, profound contemplation and strong connection with all elements of the region, she becomes intimately acquainted with many characteristics of Dalmatia, revealing its raw natural beauty, contrasting landscapes and a scintillating vigor that has always inspired all who came there.

The Austrian writer Franz Theodor Csokor referred to Paula von Preradović as the 'poet between the peoples.' This puts her among several other writers from Austria such as Herman Bahr[2] and Csokor[3] whose written opus goes beyond the surface of the attractive but incomplete picture postcard tourist image of Dalmatia. This narrow sliver of territory was part of the Austrian Empire for large parts of the 19th century, with an eventful history before it came under Habsburg rule. Before diving into the poetry of Paula von Preradović, a short historical contextualization will give an insight into a realm that inspired heliotropic Emperors, numerous Austrian artists as well as Viennese modernist playwrights with its sensory landscape.

The historical region of Dalmatia lies today in the Mediterranean part of Croatia, situated on the eastern Adriatic coast (see map pg. 89). Throughout its history, 'Dalmatia has been characterized less as an ethnic or national entity but rather more as a territorial and cultural realm."[4] A narrow maritime strip characterized by a fractured, island-studded coastline, containing numerous picturesque historic towns on the coast that contrast sharply with its barren hinterland. The region came into the orbit of antiquity thanks to its immersion into the Mediterranean world, especially through its peninsulas and plethora of islands, bays and islets. The larger islands in the southern Dalmatia archipelago were settled by the

2 Hermann Bahr, *Dalmatinische Reise,* (Berlin: S Fischer Verlag, 1909)

3 Franz Theodor Csokor, Der Verlorene Sohn, in: *Europäische Trilogie* (Vienna: Paul Zsolnay Verlag, 1952)

4 Aleksandar Jakir and Marko Trogrlić, *Dalmatien,* in: Das Südosteuropa des Regionen, ed. OJ Schmitt and M Metzeltin (Vienna: Österreichische Akademie der Wissenschaften, 2015) 91.

ancient Greeks, as can be seen in the place names such as Issa (Vis), Pharos (Hvar) and Korkyra Melaina (Korčula). Although settled by the ancient Greeks, the name Dalmatia goes back to Roman antiquity when it became a province of the Roman Empire in 32 B.C under Emperor Augustus.

Its Latin character would remain one of its defining features throughout the centuries, being a part of the Latin arc that started in the Iberian Peninsula and spread out across the Mediterranean. The Roman Emperor Diocletian upon retirement would build his palace that is still visible in the town of Split. Following the fall of the Roman Empire in the West, the Dalmatian cities on the Adriatic coast continued to harbor the remnants of the inhabitants and civilization of the Roman Empire. Between the 7-9th century, the arrival of the Croats into the province led to the eventual creation of the first Croatian realm as written in a document from 852 by the Croatian duke Trpimir. It is still today remembered as the ancient cradle of the Croatian medieval state, which became a kingdom in the 10th century that lasted until the 12th.

By this time, the Latin world had come into contact with the Slavic world. The Latin sliver of territory, with its Roman inspired culture faced off uncertainly against the newly arrived Croats. These two worlds were eventually brought together through the Christianization of the Croats, with Pope Innocent IV granting permission in 1248 to the Croats to use their own Glagolitic script instead of Latin during mass. The sonnet *Standbild des Grgur Ninski in Split* captures the vigour of these demands for the singularity of the Croatian linguistic cause, espoused by the Dalmatian bishop whose large statue built by the Viennese trained sculptor and Secession artist Ivan Meštrović stands today near Diocletian's palace. The vacuum left by the fall of the Roman Empire as well as the distance from the Byzantine Empire would result in Dalmatia entering the early Middle Ages as a particularly contested territory.

The region was a target of the Venetian, Croatian and Hungarian claims in the early Middle Ages due to the important maritime route that the eastern Adriatic province held between the remains of the

Roman Empire in the East and Venice. For the Venetians, this was the 'firstborn province'[5] of their empire which had been symbolically conceived following a crucial battle in the year 1000 that gave the Venetians the title '*Dux Dalmatorum*' (the dukes of Dalmatia). The Dalmatian coast became a keystone part of *il Serenisima´s* overseas dominion and a part of its own memorial mythology. Its deep-water ports, islands and experienced mariners formed a significant strategic section of the Empire's shipping routes towards the East. Almost continuous rule by Venice from the early 15th century left a strong imprint on the culture of the land, most visibly on its art and architecture, literature and language. Paula's poetry carries some of these distinct dialectical words such as *riva, scoglia, trabakel* and *fisolen* that are a relic of the region's Venetian past.

Venice's principal nemesis during its rule of Dalmatia was the Ottoman Empire, which first appeared on the Adriatic in 1417. From the 15th century onwards, the Adriatic became a common in-between space ruled variously by the Ottomans, the Venetian Empire, the Ragusan Republic (Dubrovnik) and the Austrian Empire. Emerging in the 17th century as a response to Ottoman incursions, it has been argued that the first Austrian fleet were in fact the Uskoks of Senj. These ferocious sea raiders who were highly dexterous mariners that harassing enemy shipping, were seen by the von Preradović family as their ancestors,[6] which Paula refers nostalgically in the poem '*Seeräuber.*' These hardy maritime muggers hound the Venetians and are romanticised in this poem that seems to epitomise for Paula the essence of the Adriatic, for her '*der Heimat wildes Herz*- the homeland's wild heart.'

Although the Austrian Empire had an outlet on the Adriatic since the 14th century when Albert III of Görz made the Istrian

5 Larry Wolff, Venice and the Slavs of Dalmatia: the drama of the Adriatic Empire in the Venetian Enlightenment, *Slavic Review*, Vol 56, No 3 (Autumn 1997) 438.

6 Tomislav Matić's article *Žumberački uskoci i potraga Dušana Preradovića za obiteljskom prošlošću* (2022) explores how Paula's father Dušan went about searching for connections, https://hrcak.srce.hr/280888

peninsula part of the Habsburg realms, it would only be at the end of the 18th century that Austria would acquire further Adriatic territory. During the first period of Austrian rule (1797-1805), the Austrian Emperor Francis I added the title 'King of Dalmatia' to his official title of Austrian Emperor. Following the fall of the Venetian Empire in 1797, in acquiring the Venetian navy "Vienna suddenly became a maritime power."[7] The increase of territory including the "bulk of Venice's territory, navy and merchant marine, a tremendous windfall that added a new dimension to her strategic horizons."[8] Apart from being contiguous to the rest of the crownlands, these provinces would provide Austria with a far more extensive outlet to the sea.

The brief interlude before the century of Austrian rule was marked most significantly by the French Empire. It would be Napoleon's rule of Dalmatia (part of his Illyrian provinces) that abolished feudalism, built roads as well as introduced the first Croatian language newspaper. The French Emperor also brought to an end to the independence of Ragusa (Dubrovnik). What remained is evoked by several sonnets written by Preradović. This includes the town's eventful history *(St Blasius von Ragusa),* magnificent architecture *(Die Sieben Säulen)* and recalcitrant aristocracy *(Die Patrizier von Ragusa).* These sonnets go beyond exploring the splendor of the city state's past, urging the reader to reflect on the declinophobic nature of this city's present, themes as alive in the past as they are today. Despite protests by some of its proud citizens to recover Dubrovnik's independence, it would be confirmed as part of the Austrian Empire following the Congress of Vienna in 1815.

Austria came across a paradise of Mediterranean backwardness. The governor of Dalmatia Graf von Lilienberg reported to the Habsburg Emperor Francis I that the new province was a "diamond in the rough which has been treated throughout many generations as common rock, yet be fashioned into a cut

7 Sondhaus, *The Habsburg Empire and the Sea*, 1.

8 Lawrence Sondhaus, *The Habsburg Empire and the Sea-Austrian naval policy* 1797-1866, (West Lafayette: Purdue University Press, 1989) 1

diamond."[9] During the period of Austrian rule, a reform and modernization program led by Vienna contributed to developments in the realm of political representation, universal primary education and naval infrastructure, with some of its results still being visible today. This includes lighthouses, to which von Preradović dedicates one of her sonnets (*Der Leuchturm*). These shoreline candles remain as glowing signs of Austria lighting up the Adriatic, still bring comfort to ships like they did during the time of *Altosterreich*.

As the national idea grew in the latter part of the 19th century, various factors including the removal of censorship in Austria post-1848, the gradual extension of civil rights in the Habsburg Empire, as well as the emergence of the national idea led to an increasingly overt 'nationalisation' of the Adriatic sea that began in the second half of the 19th century."[10] The Italian rebirth program, the *Risorgimento*, targeted parts of the Austrian Empire as its irredemed province. The city of the lagoon "remained the home of the main naval base, academy and shipbuilding facilities between 1814-1848 and Italian was the language of command in the fleet and of instruction at the naval academy."[11] Italian speakers, most of them Venetian, dominated the officer corps and provided the bulk of the sailors to the enlarged Austrian Navy.

Following a revolt in 1848 when large parts of the Italian speaking officer corps rebelled, the Austrian principal Austrian naval base would be moved to the Istrian port of Pula. It would be Paula's grandfather, the Croatian writer Petar Preradović who served in these campaigns, fighting as an officer in the Austrian army in the same campaigns that the fictional hero of Radetsky

9 Wenzel Vetter Graf von Lilienberg, *Roher Diamant Dalmatien: Die habsburgische Verwaltung, ihre Probleme und das Land, wie beschrieben von seinem Gouverneur Lilienberg für Kaiser Franz I.* (1834)

10 Borhut Klabjan, The scramble for the Adriatic. *Austrian history journal* 42, Minnesota 2011, 18.

11 Lawrence Sondhaus, *The Austro-Hungarian naval officer corps,* Austrian History Yearbook 24, 1993, 52.

March von Trotta fights against Italian irredentists who were gnawing on the Austrian Empire. As Garibaldi and his Red Shirts conquered Sicily and Naples in 1860, the fall of the city touched off a panic in Vienna over the security of their access to the sea. Austria "feared that Garibaldi and his followers would attempt to repeat their recent success with a revolutionary landing in Istria and Dalmatia."[12]

Italian irredentists on the Eastern Adriatic coast, conscious of the Latin and Venetian heritage along the Austrian littoral hoped to incorporate Istria, Trieste and Dalmatia into the new Italian kingdom with outside help. Otto von Bismarck encouraged the nascent Italian state to carry out an "invasion of Dalmatia in 1866 and Moltke encouraged an assault on Trieste."[13] The Italian government, on a roll after victories against Austria in 1848 and 1859 aimed to "reduce Austria to a land locked country"[14] by sending its navy to the Dalmatian Island of Vis in the mid-Adriatic. But the Habsburg Navy's resounding victory at Vis in 1866 in the "second largest naval battle in the 19th century after Trafalgar"[15] resulted in Austria gaining "unprecedented, unquestioning hegemony over the Adriatic."[16] The stability afforded by the peace coincided with technological innovations that helped develop the Dalmatian coast that by this time had become a crownland of the Austrian Empire.

Despite the lack of a rail link between the capital and the Dalmatian coast, the emergence of the steamboat, allowed ships to more reliably following a timetable thanks to inventions that facilitated this and resulted in a much more connected Adriatic realm. The steamship company Austrian Lloyd was founded in 1833 and

12 Lawrence Sondhaus, *The Habsburg Empire and the sea-Austrian naval policy 1797-1866*, (West Lafayette: Purdue University Press, 1989) 203.

13 Sondhaus, *The Habsburg empire and the sea*, 252.

14 Ibid, 259.

15 Josip Vrandečić, *Dalmatinski autonomistički pokret u XIX stoljeću* (Zagreb: Dom i svijet, 2002) 136.

16 Sondhaus, *The Habsburg empire and the sea*, 259.

the opening of the increased naval traffic on the Eastern Adriatic meant that this strange and unknown land became more accessible to travelers, artists and tourists. The beginnings of tourism coincide with an artistic turnaround and new aesthetic understandings. While Van Gogh and Paul Signac painted fishing boats on the *Côte d'Azur*, Austria's artists Egon Schiele, Emil Jakob Schindler and Albin Egger Lienz capture similar southern serenity in the southern parts of what had also become the Adriatic monarchy. *Fin-de-siecle* Dalmatia would see the opening one of the first modern hotels 1897, a project initiated by Baron Victor Kalchberg, the chairman of the Austria Lloyd shipping company. The Grand Hotel Imperial, designed by Viennese architect Ludwig Tischler, was the first place in Dubrovnik that had the electric light-bulb installed.

In 1913, Austria celebrated the centenary of the Habsburg's rule of the province with a lavish exhibition in Vienna that celebrated and showcased the best of the Empire's most southern province. In the same year, Egon Schiele, the Austrian expressionist painter, inspired by frequent trips to the Adriatic as von Preradović, painted '*Versinkende Sonne,*' capturing the tense and tender twilight years of the Habsburg monarchy. Schiele's friend and art critic Arthur Roessler is said to have commented 'in front of the sun it is already dark and cold, every leaf on the branch is stiff and numb from the cold. A deeply melancholic sky makes me ask whether this same sun will ever return.' This revealing commentary on a painting that seemed to indicate a fateful destiny turned out to be prophetic.

The collapse of the Austro-Hungarian Empire brought to an end an epoch that had marked not just Dalmatia but the rest of the Adriatic. A secret treaty signed by the Entente powers in London in 1915 meant that it would be occupied by Italy for several years in the post-bellum period and only the intervention of the American President Woodrow Wilson meant that the treaty was annulled as it was seen as a form of 'old world diplomacy' that had no place in Wilson's new order. After 1918, the larger part of Dalmatia would become part of the new south Slav state, the

Kingdom of the Serbs, Croats and Slovenes. It would disappear as an administrative entity, losing its elected Diet as well as its status as a *Königreich* (crownland) of the Austrian Empire.

The Second World War saw the lion's share of Dalmatia being occupied by fascist Italy, who used its Roman and Venetian cultural heritage as well as previous diplomatic promises of the Entente powers as a justification of including the region in its new Mediterranean Empire.

After the Second World War, Dalmatia became part of the Federal people's republic of Yugoslavia, within the federal entity of Croatia. The post-1945 period would be characterised by urbanisation, industrialisation and the increase in the importance of tourism for the region that has remained a significant source of income up to today. At the beginning of the 1990s, with Croatia becoming an independent republic as a result of democratic elections, Dalmatia would become part of Croatia. The state would enter the EU in 2013.

Vicko Marelić, Korčula, December 2023

Ausfahrt

O Meer! O altes Meer im Mittagslicht,
In tausend Nächten allzu wild begehrtes,
Ich sehe wieder dein durch nichts versehrtes
Hinblauen ohne Makel und Gewicht.

Dein Atem kühlt mir wieder das Gesicht,
Dein Salz küsst meinen Mund als langentbehrtes
Hulldzeichen, da ein endlich heimgekehrtes
Verbanntes Herz zu seiner Mutter spricht.

Zum Hafenausgang hat das Schiff gewendet,
Die ersten Möwen nahn mit Lichtem Schrei,
Als ob der offne Himmel sie gesendet,

Und an der Insel weissen Felsenbrüsten
Und an des Festland jungen Wein vorbei
Geht sanft die Fahrt nach den geträumten Küsten.

Anchors Away!

Dear sea! O venerable sea in the midday glows
Wildly desired, for a thousand nights
I see you again, your immaculate sights,
of spotless azure, where no burden or flaw flows

Your breath always refreshes my face.
Your salt kisses my mouth, like a long yearned for
Homage, that final return to a shore
Of a banished heart embracing its mother's grace

The ship tacks towards the port's end
Sea gulls flying and clamoring near by
As if by the very heavens sent.

Sailing by the island's steep white cliffs of yore
We voyage where the nascent vineyards lie
Cruising gently to the dreamed-up Illyrical shore

Lob der Insel Rab

Wer säh an deinem Umriss je sich satt,
Dem steil hinragenden in Gesicht und Stürme,
Du in der weissen Vierzahl deiner Türme
Aufs Vorgebirge hingestufte Stadt?

Du Starkummauerte und Schlankerbaute,
Du überlebende aus Pest und Tod,
Du Ersterglühende in Morgenrot,
Von feuchter Nebelnacht zuletzt Umgraute!

Wer, in der Inserlflur Verschollenheit,
Den warmen Mulden, dicht vom Wein und Myrte,
Erkennte reuig nicht, wie arm er irrte

Im Lärm der Welt? Wer spürte nicht im Bogen
Der Buchten, mandelblütenüberschneit,
Die Masse Gottes, selig ausgewogen?

A Praise of Rab

Who could ever tire, looking at your shape,
Protruding steeply into foams and storms,
Your vast number of white tower forms
Standing tall on the steep-staired cape

You, strongly walled, slender structured sight
Survivor of plagues and demise
The first illuminator at sunrise
Smothered in greyness after a foggy night

Who, marooned in the island fields cast away
In the sizzling hollows flowing with wine and myrrh
Penitently would not see the wretched wanderings

In the world's clamor, who could not sense the curved bow's
Bays, sprinkled, snow-like with blossoming almond trees,
The Almighty's measures, blissfully balanced

Der Leuchturm

Aus dem Scoglio steigt fein weißes Ragen.
Seine Lampensonne, glasumdacht,
Muß, den Tod zu bannen, Nacht um Nacht
Grünes Blinken durch das Dunkel jagen.

Unter um den runden Fuß des Turmes
Läuft ein Streifen Strandes, kleben Häuser.
Ein Geschlecht von Wächtern, wie Kartäuser
Hart, wohnt hier. Im Wehn des Borastrumes

In der schattenlosen Sommer Brennen
Wachsen braune Knaben auf, die kaum
Film und Fußball aus Gerüchten kennen.

Wissen nur um Muscheln, Möwen, Schiffe,
Wind und Ferne. Daß auf ihrem Rifffe
Eine Kiefer grüne, ist ihr Traum

Lighthouse

From the rocky reef soars a fine white tower.
With its precious, glass roofed light,
That keeps death at bay, night after night.
Chasing darkness away by a flashing green flower.

Under the round foot of the light's limbs
Where houses stick out on a sliver of beach
Dwells a dynasty of hardy lighthouse keepers,
Like Carthusian monks against the wind

In the shadeless summer days
Tanned lads grow, who barely sees.
With films or football just a haze

Their reef world is but mussels, gulls and ships.
With wind and high seas on their lips
Dreaming merely of green pine trees

Incoronate

Ihr Inselschwärme, lichtes Traumgesicht,
Ihr Inselkränze, Kahler Inselreih'n,
Unzählbar lieget ihr im Sonnenschein,
Ganz ohne Tier und Baum und Erdenschicht.

Gott schuf das Licht, und gab euch neunmal Licht,
Er machte euch aus knochenbelichem Stein
Und liess türkisenblaue Wasser sein
Um euren Rand. Doch mehr tat Gott euch nicht.

Weissleuchtend wie am dritten Schöpfungstag
Ruht ihr im Meere, grossen Blumen gleich,
Ruht ihr in Salzgeruch und Wellenschlag,

Errötend, wenn die Sonne kommt und geht,
Wie Keuschgebliebene an Gnade reich
In eurer Armut karger Majestät.

Kornati Isles

Island swarms, tonsured dream faces
Wreaths and rows of bare island
Infinite, you all lie in the sun
Shorn of animal, tree or soil

The Almighty made light, gifting you light
Crafting you from pale as bone stone
'Let there be, turquoise blue sea
around your edges' More He did not do

You gleam bright white, as on the Third day of Creation
Reposing in the sea, just like large flowers
Resting in the salty scent and whirls of the waves

Blushing when the sun rises and sets
Just as those remaining chaste in the grace
In the dearth of your barren majesty.

Karstplateau

Kahler denn dieses ist kein Mondgefild
Es können Steine fahler nirgends bleichen
Und durftiger Wurzeln nicht herniederrreichen
Zum Felsenspalt, mit trocknem Staub gefüllt.

Und nichts kann greller blenden, denn dies wild
Entbrannte Himmelsblauen ohne Gleichen,
Der Harten Bora steil gewölbtes Zeichen,
Blauer denn blau und ewig ungestillt

Auf Eseln naht sich, bäuerlich schwarz umtan,
Aufrechter Reiterinnen eine Zeile
Spindeln in Hände, sehn sie fremd dich an

Von Wochenmarkt im Weißen Šibenik
Kehren die Königlichen ohne Eile
In ihrer Hütten Urweltnot zurück.

Karst Plateau

No moonscape is as bleak as this
Nowhere are stones bleached so sallow
And thirstier roots in no place reach so shallow
To the dry, dust filled crag.

And nothing so piercingly glares
Than this wildly inflamed singular sky,
Or the bitter Bora's steeply carved tag,
Bluer than azure and eternally unquenched

Approaching on a donkey, rustically clad in black
A row of uptight mounted women
Spindle in hand, they look at you, the outsider

From the weekly market in white Šibenik
Without a rush the regal return
To the primordial hardship of their shacks.

Homerische Ölbaum

Baum des Odysseus, Ölbaum, lichter Baum
Du leidst Beil und Schnitt, um in den Tagen
Des späten Herbst die runde Frucht zu tragen,
Baum des Odysseus, heilig lichter Baum.

Da den Gejagten spät der salzige Schaum
Der Wasser doch nach Ithaka verschalgen,
Tief schlafend, wie es uns die Lieder Sagen,
Da grüsstest du als erster ihn, o Baum.

Du standest da, noch eh Athene kam,
Die Schönverwandelte. Du standest schmal
Und hoch und silbern blinkend, während lahm

Der König lag in seinem schweren Schlaf.
Doch als den Blick er hob zum ersten Mal,
Warst du es, den sein Duderauge traf.

Homeric Olive Tree

Tree of Odysseus, olive tree, bare tree,
Suffering hatchet and cuts, to bear round fruit
In the late days of Fall,
Tree of Odysseus, holy sparse tree.

For as the hounded was finally on the sea's salty foam
Waters to Ithaca brought,
Deeply asleep as the epic recalls
O olive tree, you were the first to greet him.

You stood there, even before the (Goddess) Athena,
This beautiful apparition. You stood trim
and high and silverly gleaming, whilst hamstrung

The King lay in his deep sleep.
Yet as he raised his eyes for the first time,
It was you whom his patient eye beheld.

Trogir

Aus süssen Südens offner Landschaft lacht
Das Tempelrund, indes mit Saurierlenden
Und Riesenhaupt starr von der Riva Enden
Das Camerlengoschloss die Stadt bewacht.

O Trogir, Traum aus Grellheit und aus Nacht!
O deiner breiten Reede Sonnenblenden
Und deiner tiefen Tore schwarzes Wenden
Und deines Doms dämonendunkle Pracht.

Die Schlitze deiner Dämmergassen ziehn
Vorbei an adeligen Sopraporten
Zum Wunder deines weissen Platzes hin,

Wo aus den glatten Fliesen lichtumbebt,
Jenseits von allen Bildern, Liedern, Worten
Der reine Gottespfeil des Turms sich hebt.

Trogir

From the sweet south vast vista chuckles
the roundness of the temple, whilst saurian loins and
A giant head grown stiff at the end of the Riva
guards the Kamerlengo fortress in the town.

Oh Trogir, nighttime dazzling dream!
With your broad, sun shaded anchorages
Your deep gates turning black
And your cathedral, its devilishly dark glory

Those slits in your lanes at dusk roll
Past the noble overdoor
To the marvel of your white main square

Where from the slick, light-glimmering
Indescribable, beyond all images, songs, words
Rises God's pure arrow from the tower

Nacht-Ritt auf das Vorgebirge

Es klagt aus der versunkenen Meeresbucht
Der Ruf der Fischer, nächtig, sagenalt
Doch älter noch, verrucht und hungrig, schallt
Die Antwort der Schakale aus der Schlucht.

Da Josef und die Jungfrau auf der Flucht
Das Kind verbargen, Wüste war und Wald
Nicht öder da, noch schauriger durchhallt
Denn dieses Fels-Tals gnadelose Wucht.

Auf steilem Passweg schweift mit seinen Schafen
Ein scheuer Hirt. Die Eselinnen gehen
Ganz sacht durchs Steinicht, drin die Vipern schlafen

Bald aber werden, frei von Graus und Mühe,
Vom Bergeskamm wir lichte Inseln sehen
Im blassen Vorweltblau der ersten Frühe.

Nighttime Ride to the Forelands

A wail rings out from the sunken bays
The fishermen, their nightly age-old songs
Older still, hideous and hungry responds
The jackals from the valley

Neither Joseph and Mary's flight
With the child, through desert and forest
Was bleaker or eerier echoing
Than this rocky valley's merciless force

On the steep mountain pass rambling with his sheep
A shy shepherd. While the donkeys
Tread carefully where the viper sleep

Soon we will see, free from horror and trouble
From the top of the mountain ridge the shorn islands
In the pale, dusk of the morning

Trabakel

Es fahren die Fischer um Schombri heut aus.
Borin bläht die blutrot bemalten Lateiner;
Im Frischen der Brise wird blässer und kleiner
Die Kiefer der Küste, des Zollwächers Haus.

Es schlagen die Segel beim Reffen und Wenden.
Es feuern die Männer, sie kochen und keuern
Am Boden des Bootes beim Wein und den sauern
Fisolen, getreulich die Taue in Händen.

Zum Abend, da müssen die Netze sie heben
Von schuppichtem Zappeln, von filbrigem Leben
Ist blinkend die bauchige Barke bewohnt.

Heimkehren die Müden in Traumesgedanken.
So schwartz wie der Wein, den die Durftigen tranken,
Erdunkelt ihr Segel im finkenden Mond.

Trabakel [17]

The fishermen are off today for the *Scombri*[18]
As the *Burin*[19] blows the blood red painted Lateen rig
In the freshness of the breeze the coastal pines and custom house
Pale and become smaller.

The sails thump as they shorten and turn,
The crew loosen them, as they crouch and cook.
On the boat's deck with wine and sour
Fazolice, faithfully with ropes in hand

In the evening they must raise the nets.
With flakey fidgeting silverish life
That inhabits the boat, flashing bountifully

The tired turn back home in dreamy thoughts
Blackened as the wine that the thirsty drank.
Darkening their sails by the sinking moon

17 Sailing fishing boat

18 Mackrel in local dialects

19 From Bora, the stormy north wind, Burin is its lighter version.

Isthmus

Ins heisse Flimmern prallen Mittags sticht
Der steile Bergeskepel spitz hinein,
Dem einen Zackengürtel bleich wie Bein
Die Türkenmauer um die Hüfte flicht

Mit blauem Feuer stürtz das Über-Licht
Des Sommertags auf seinen Gipfel ein.
Blau zittert grünes Kraut, blau fahler Stein.
Der Berg zerbicht des Himmels Glocke nicht.

Doch unten läuft die Strasse weissumloht,
Läuft grell und staubig hin von Meer zu Meer.
Und wo sie starben einst den Türkentod,

Dort trabt ein Maultier, fliegenübersät.
Es trägt an einem breiten Greife schwer,
Um den gestärkt der Linnenkittel steht.

Neck of land

Into the hot flickering of the blazing noon
Piques sharply the steep crest,
Braided round the cliffs crag is the Turkish wall
Like a belt of spikes pale as bones

With blue fire the thrusts the great light
Of the summer days on its high peak.
Blued up green weeds tremble, bleak blue stone
The mountain breaks not heaven's bell like cover

Yet underneath runs the road clothed in white
Running glaringly and dusty sea to sea
Where they once died the Turkish death

There trots a mule, ridden with flies
Laden with a broad heavy old man
Around which is bound a linen gown.

Der Guslar

Den braunen Hirtenmantel ausgebreitet
Sitzt wirren Haars der Alte auf den Steinen,
Indes er zittrig streichend auf der einen
Saite der Gusla sein Gedicht begleitet.

Er singt das Lied vom König Vukašin,
Wie er der Vila Hemd geraubt und Krone
Beim Kolotanz. Vom starken Königssohne
Marko, dem Helden, singt er vor sich hin.

Unzählige Lieder weiss er, lang und schwer,
Und singt sie frei mit unbeirrtem Munde.
Sein Enkelsohn jedoch, der lesen kann,

Kauft aus der Händlertasche schmierigem Grunde
Kalenderschwatz und Kriminalroman
Bald kennt die alten Lieder keiner mehr.

The Guslar

Spreading out the brown herdsman cloak
The tangled haired oldie sits on the stones,
As he quivers and strums the
String of the *gusla*[20] backing his poem.

He sings to a song of King Vukašin[21]
How he stole the fairy's shirt and crown
At the Kolo[22] dance. Of the mighty king's son
Marko, the hero, he sings to himself.

Countless songs he knows, long and hard,
He sings them by heart, unflinching mouth.
Yet his grandson, who can read,

Buys from the greasy grounds of the sales bag
Calendar chit chat and crime novels.
Soon, no one will know the old songs.

---

20 Traditional instrument from the Balkans

21 Serbian king Vukašin Mrnjačević

22 Kolo is a traditional circular dance present in south-eastern Europe.

Standbild des Grgur Ninski in Split (Ivan Meštrović) i

Du stehst gebogen, Bischof, Riese, Mann,
Wie eine Sehne, die der Pfeil gespannt,
Und der gereckte Finger deiner Hand
Tut allen Widerfachern Drohung an.

Ob du auch milde priesterlich umtan
Mit faltig falllend geistlichem Gewand,
Da war kein König, der so herrlich stand,
So Kämpferisch und keinem untertan.

Du hältst das Buch, um das dein langer Kampf
Mit allen Mächten dieser Erde ging,
In deiner Linken in gewaltigem Krampf.

Dein Mund steht auf, der vieles Harte sprach
Und kühner Rede zäh sich unterfing:-
Die Könige und Rom selbst gaben nach.

Statue of Grgur Ninski (Ivan Meštrović) (i)

You stand tall, bent outward, Bishop, Giant, Man,
Like a string pulled back by the arrow,
The elongated finger of your hand
Threatening all foes

Even though you are clemently frocked
With wrinkled, falling ecclesiastical vestures,
No king stood like you, so gloriously,
So pugnaciously and indominantly

In your left hand you hold the book
Long fought for, against all temporal forces
In a fierce, unshakable grip

Your mouth open, speaking with fiery tongue
and stoutly ventured with audacious talk
Even the King and Rome themselves surrendered.

Standbild des Grgur Ninski in Split (Ivan Meštrović) (ii)

Wenn du, vom Zwang des Postaments entlasten,
Herniederstiegelst in den grossen Falten
Des Bischofskelides: welche Ängste malten
Sich in den Mienen da, und welch Erblassen!

Du gingest erzern dröhend durch die Gassen,
Und wo du streiftest, rieselts in dem alten
Gemäuer. Kinder würden festgehalten,
Dass es sie lüste nicht, dich anzufassen.

Dein Haupt im starren Haar, es schwebte hoch,
Wo schon die Dächer sind. Des Angesichts
Zornvolle Steile dräute immer noch

Dein Fuss in der Sandale riesenhalft,
Er schritte eilends, und ihm hemmte nichts.
Und Split erzitterte vor deine Kraft.

Statue of Grgur Ninski (Ivan Meštrović) (ii)

Whenever you, freed from the pedestals force.
Stooped into the great creases
Of the Bishops frocks: their countenances
Paled up with unspeakable fear!

You went steely and roaringly though the lanes
Wherever you roamed, the old ruins still flutter.
Children would be held tight,
So that they would not crave touching you.

Your head in stiff hair, it swarmed high,
Where even the roofs are. The visages
wrathful slants still looming by

Your foot in the sandal- colossal
Strode hastily, nothing hindered him
As Split trembled from your vigour.

Die Sieben Säulen
(Rectorenpalast zu Dubrovnik)

Blattgekraus das erste Kapitell
Auf dem zweiten Frazenblick aus Zweigen,
Während nackte Puttenleiber reigen
Auf den mittlern dreien, marmorhell

Mühend sich, den schweren Früchterstrauss
Mit den kleinen Händen festzubinden,
Und sich schleppend unter Herbstgewinden.
Auf dem sechsten wieder Blattgekraus.

Auf dem letzten thront, - ein Alchemiste,
Faustisch mit Retort und Rattenzahn,
Äsculap, der alte Gott der Küste,

Während faltig angetane Städter,
Opfernd mit dem Säckel, mit dem Hahn,
Nahn von jenseits der Akanthusblätter.

The Seven Pillars
(of the Rector's palace in Dubrovnik)

Crinkly leafed up the first column
From the second a grimace glances from twigs
While naked cherubs dance round
On the middle three, marble bright

Struggling to bundle the heavy fruit bunch
With their small hands
Dragging themselves under the autumn wreath
On the already sixth leafy bundle

On the last one throning, - an alchemist
Faustian with retort and rat tooth
Asclepius, the old God of the coast

Whilst wrinkly clothed gentlemen,
Sacrificing bag in hand, with the rooster
Approaching from beyond the acanthus leaves

Abend in Dominikaner Kreuzgang (Dubrovnik)

Das Himmelsviereck überm Hof aus Stein
Ist ganz erfüllt vom überstürzten Jagen
Nachtschwarzer Schwalben, die so schwirrend klagen,
Wie Seelen, unerlöst vom Höllenpein.

Nur manchmal eine flüchtet sich herein,
Wo in des frühen Mai's geliebten Tagen
Orangenbäume Frucht und Blüten tragen,
Und flieht schon wieder mit entsetztem Schrein.

Die weissen Mönche aber, müden Schuhs,
Gehn an der Balustrate hin und wieder
Und beten tief geneigt den Angelus.

Und ihrer einer naht sich wie im Traum,
Lässt in den Brunnen tief den Eimer nieder
Und tränkt voll Liebe den Oragenbaum.

Evening in Dominican Cloister

The celestial quad over the stone court
Abounds in hurried hunters
Swallows dark as night, so whirlingly wail,
Like souls, unredeemed from the torments of hell

Only at times one flees in,
Where in early mays beloved days
Orange trees blossom and fruits bear
And fleeing again with a startling cry

Yet the while monks, of tired foot,
Go along the Balustrade at times
And deeply bowed, they pray the Angelus.

Dream like one of them draws nearer,
Lowers deeply down the bucket
And lovingly waters the orange tree.

St Blasius von Ragusa (i)

Seht ihn, der die Stadt gerettet hat.
Seht den Heiligen, der allerorten
An den Kapitellen, Mauern, Pforten
Streng gemeisselt thront als Herr der Stadt.

Mit dem Stabe und der Bischofmütze
Immer armebreitend Sveti Vlah
Wogt barock auf seiner Kirche Dach,
Äugt vom Pile-Tor, dass er es schütze.

Mächtig prangt er an der Münze Front,
Vom Altare blinkt er silbern her.
Doch am runden Ivansturme wohnt

Er am liebsten. Unter Bootsmannspfiffen
Ragt er ob den Molen, Bojen, Schiffen,
Hält die Hände bannend übers Meer.

St Blasius of Ragusa (i)

Behold him, who saved the town
Behold the saint, who everywhere
On the pillars, walls, gates
Sharply carved enthroned as the Lord of the town

With the staff and the Bischop's Mitre
Sveti Vlaho, always spreading arms
Surges baroquely on the roof of his church
Peering from the Pile gate, to protect it.

How mightily he shines from the front of coin
From the altars he silverly gleams
Yet on the round Ivan tower he

Prefers to dwell. Under the boatswain whistles
He looms over the harbour moles, buoys, ships,
Holding his hands averting over the sea.

St Blasius von Ragusa (ii)

Hört nun, wie er seine Stadt bewacht,
Der, die Türken spürend, sein Gebeine
Jählings riss aus dem Reliquienschreine,
Sturm zu läuten in der Boranacht

Der vom Strang nicht liess die Knochenhand,
Bis die Wachen, schnarchend hingefunken,
Und die Bürger, karnevalestrunken,
Schaudernd sich ernüchtert und ermannt,

Und sie alle nun in Fackelgrelle
Stürzen übern hallenden Stradon
Zu den Stücken auf die äussern Wälle,

Heulend irr zum oft verratnen Gotte.
Denn es bog die Sarazenenflotte
Schwarz und lautlos um Lacroma schon

St Blasius of Ragusa (ii)

Hear now, how he guards his town,
He, who sensing the Turks, abruptly
snatched his remains from the reliquary casket
Ringing the bells in the stormy Bora night

He who could not take his bony hand off the bell ringer
Until the watchmen, snoringly sagged,
And the townsfolk, carnival giddy,
Suddenly sobered and arose,

And they all in the glare of torches
Descend on the clamoring *Stradun*[23]
Onto the chunks of the outer ramparts,

Weeping frantically to the often-betrayed God
For the Saracen fleet already sailed around Lokrum-
Black and silent.

23 Main pedestrian street in the historic part of Dubrovnik

Die Patrizier von Ragusa

Ihre Häuser stürzen zu Ruinen,
Ohne Dächter stehn die stolzen da,
Wenn nicht jenes Schlimmere geschah,
Dass sich fremde Hand erfrecht nach ihnen.

Keine Erben wurden mehr geboren
In die Knechtschaft, wie's Marmont zum Trotze
Die Ghetaldi, Bonda, Pozza, Gozze
Anno Achzehnhundertacht geschworen.

Enkel ihrer freigelassen Kmeten,
Fremde, Gasser, Lumpenhunde treten
Jetzt das heilige Pflaster des Stradon.

Doch die Alten, nie gebeugte Seele,
(Alle sind nun bald versammelt schon)
Schlafen auf dem Friedhof San Michele.

The Ragusan Nobles

Their houses fell to ruins
Roofless the proud ones remain,
If not the even worse happened
Than outsiders hand dares grab them.

No longer were heirs born
Into servitude, in defiance of Marmont,
Thus Ghetaldi, Bonda, Pozza, Gozze
In the year 1808 vowed

Now the grandchildren of their freed serfs,
Foreigners, gawkers and louse stroll
On the hallowed cobbles of the *Stradun*

Yet the old, of indomitable soul
(almost now wholly assembled)
Sleep in St Michael's cemetery

Herrenhaus bei Canosa

Dies ist kein Haus mehr, keines Menschen Statt.
Diest ist ein Schmuckschrein, eitel hingestelt,
Ein totes Ding am letzten Rand der Welt,
Das keine Wurzeln mehr im Blute hat.

Und es ist nicht mehr Erfuhrt, was sich matt
Um diese Schätze drängt. Und was sie hält
In den Vitrinen wunderlich gestellt,
Ist Liebe nicht mehr, noch erfüllte Tat.

Selbst die Gespenster wohnen hier nicht mehr,
Die vordem kamen, vom Geruch verführt
Verwesten Krames. Ihnen graut zu sehr

Vor einer Hülse, so wie diese taub,
Die, von lebendigem Finger angerührt,
Zu Asche fiele und zu trübem Staub.

Manor House upon Canosa

This is a house no more, no human dwells here.
This splendid shrine, put up with conceit,
A dead being at the end of the world,
With no more roots in its blood

There is no longer awe, that dimly
Crowds around these treasures. And what is keeping
Them strangely joined together in the showcase is
No longer love, or fulfilled deed any more

Even the ghosts don't live here anymore,
For those who came before, allured by the scent
Of decaying clutter. They, too terrified

By this shell, as they also were numbed
As when touched by a living finger
Falling to ashes and dust

Vorspruch I

Ihr Riesenhaften, Gottes ernte Boten,
Noch nie ward euer dämmerndes Gesicht
Herabgezwungen so ins Tageslicht,
Wie's hier geschah. Denn dies: wie ihr der Toten

Kindkleine Seelen haltet in den Armen,
Harte Vollstrecker göttlichem Gebot,
Doch wissen um den bitteren Menschentod,
Die gottgewohnten Augen voll Erbarmen,

Das ahnte keiner. Botticelli nicht,
Da er den grossentflammten Gabriel
Zur Jungfrau in die Halle eilen liess,

Noch Buonarotti, der vors Paradies
Mit seinem Schwert aus Härte und aus Licht
Hintreten liess den reisigen Michael

Prologue I

You gigantic, stern messengers of God
Never before has your dawning face
Been forced down into the light of day
As happened here. For this, as you hold

In your arm the child-sized souls of the dead,
Rigorous executors of divine command
Yet aware of the bitter human death
Merciful eyes, wont to God

This no one sensed. Not Botticeli,
For he had led loose the fiercely ablaze Gabriel
Hasten to the virgin into the hall,

Neither Buonarroti, at the gates of Paradise,
Had Michael, with his sword beweaponed
made from rigour and light

Prologue II

Und auch der Bruder nicht aus Fiesole
Hat es gewusst, ob er sie gleich in Scharen
Hinwachsen liess in ihren hellen Haaren
Mit Notenblatt, Fagott und Oboe.

Denn jene Engel, leidensledige
Botschaftbesteller, lieblich unerfahren
In Schmerz und Schuld, sind grausam von Gebaren
Wie selige Kinder und so kühl wie Schnee.

Doch ihr vier Engel: was euch Gott esparte,
Geburt und Tod und Menschenwandels harte
Not und Beschmutzung, - dunkel sieht man's stehn

Auf eurer Stirnen ungeahnten Bogen
Und dass, eh ihr das leere All Durchflogen,
Ihr Gott von Angesichte habt gesehn.

Prologue II

Neither the brother not from Fiesole
Knew not, if he would let her
Grow wildly in droves with her fair hair
Musical score, bassoon and oboe

For those Angels, painless
Message summoners, sweetly callow
In pain and guilt, cruel in behavior
Just like blessed children, cold, as snow.

Yet you four angels; what God spared you
Birth, death and the twists of man, hard
Misery and stains, darkly it stands there

On your brows unimagined Arches
And that, before you flew through the empty heavens
You have seen the face of God.

Engel des Sohnes

Schwebender Fuss des Engels rechts vom Tor!
Er ist noch erdnah. Doch er wird sich heben
Sehr schnell und wird durch Dunst und Wolken schweben
Und gleiten in den leeren Raum empor.

Aus faltenlosem Engelskleid hervor
Ragen die Fergenarme und umgeben
Die nackte Seele, die in Frost und Beben
Sich drängend wendet an des Engels Ohr.

O um den Tod, den erst erlitten Tod!
O um den Abschied und die schwarze Flut,
Die alles nahm! O um die letzte Not!

Mein Engel, sieh, ich zittre noch so sehr.
Ihr Arme, haltet ihr mich fest und gut,
Indes wir fliegen übers dunkle Meer!

The Son's Angel

Hovering angel's foot on the gates right!
Still close to earth he is. Yet he will rise
swiftly and hover through haze and clouds
And sliding upwards in the empty room.

From the angel's uncreased gown
Stick out the ferryman's arms and veil
The naked soul, that turns to the angel's ear
With urgency in thrust and quiver.

Woe death newly suffered death!
Woe farewell and the black flood,
That took everything! Woe ultimate misery!

My angel, look how much I still tremble.
Your arms, hold me tight and well,
While we fly over the dark sea?

Engel Der Tochter

Du linken Engels schweigendes Gesicht,
Zu fremdem Todesschweiss herabgesenktes,
Durch fremden Abschiedsjammer mitgekränktes,
Mitfürchtendes das baldige Gericht.

Unnennbar noch wie gerner Monde Licht
Um deine Stirn von Gottes Blinken hängt es
Und um die Wölbung deiner Wangen drängt es
Von Seinem Anhauch noch und lässt dich nicht.

Die Seele, die du hältst, umflicht in Schauern,
Die allzujunge, deinen Bruderhals.
Da träuft in ihre Sterbequal dein Trauern,

Wien in das Qualmen wüster Feuersbrände
Das kühle Sprühen eines Wafferstrahls.
Und tief getröstet faltet sie die Hände.

The Daughter's Angel

You left angel's silent face,
Sunk into the unknown death sweat,
Hurt by distant farewell wailings,
The imminent judgement in fear

Unnamable still-like the distant moonlight
Hanging around your brow of God's glances
And around the arch of your cheeks it shoves
By the Almighty's whiff, still, not letting go

The all too young soul that you hold,
Entangled in awe, your brother's neck
There gives off her agony, your sorrow,

As in the wild firebrands smoldering
The cool spraying of a drizzling water spurt
Deeply solaced, she clasps her hands

Die Engel Der Eltern I

Ihr Aufwärtsschauenden in Tempels Tiefe,
Ist jemand, der in euren hoch gebogenen
Armen die Seele nisten säh, verflognen
Singvögeln gleich, und den's nicht überliefe,

Zu schweben so wie sie, euch dicht umfassend,
Verschaut in eure lohend Gesichter,
Das alte Land des Lärmes und der Lichter
In steilem Fluge immer tiefer lassend?

Wie ruht des Vaters Seele sanft sich aus!
Ihm gellen noch im Ohr der Stapelläufe
Gedröhn und Pfeifen, seilschende Verkäufe

Und seines eignene Mundes Machtbefehle.
Nun aber schliesst sich dunkelnd das Gebraus.
Gottnähe überschweigt die Mannesseele.

The Parent's Angel I

You who look up in the temple's depth
Is there someone who saw the souls nestling
In your highly curved arms, like fading
Songbirds, who would not be overrun

To float just like them, holding you closely
Smitten by your blazing faces,
The old country of noise and lights
In steep flights always deeper letting?

How gently does the father's soul rest!
The shrills and the whistles of the ship's launch
Still in the ear, the sails haggling

And commands given by his own mouth
Now the roar darkly comes to an end
Near to God, over silencing the man's soul

Die Engel Der Eltern II

Die Mutter spricht: drei Tode starb ich schon,
Dreimal erlitt ich Todes-Schweiss und Ringen,
Da in der Seuche Drangsal alle gignen,
Der Mann, die Tochter und der junge Sohn.

Nun trage, Engel, eilends mich davon.
Mein Tod, er ist mir süsser denn Syringen,
Ich höre schon die hohne Glocken klingen
Und die Geliebten, o, sie nahen schon.

Ist es noch weit? Ich sah sie schon so nah.
Nun find sie wieder ferne und verschwommen,
Und meine Tränen sind noch immer da.

Tu deinen Arm, mein Engel, dichter her,
Dass ich noch raste, eh wir heim gekommen.
Ich bin so müde und ich kann nicht mehr.

The Parent's Angel II

The mother speaks: three deaths I have died
Three times I have suffered death's sweat and struggles
As all went into the epidemic's tribulation,
My husband, my daughter and the young son

Now carry me, Angel, hurry me towards
My death, is sweeter to me than syringes
I already hear the bells toll for me
And my beloved, oh they are nearer.

Is it so far? I see them already so near.
Now they are again far and hazy,
And my tears are still here.

Make your arm, my angel, thicker,
For I am still resting, as we come home
I am so tired, I cannot go on any more.

OTHER POEMS BY
PAULA VON PRERADOVIĆ

Istrianische Landschaft

Der Hirte singt, die Wolke loht.
Die Heide liegt im Abendrot.
Die Heide duftet weit und breit
Nach Thymian und Einsamkeit
Es droht die Stadt von ferne her,
Und an den Hügeln bleicht das Meer

Istrian Landscape

The shepherd sings, the clouds ablaze.
The heath spread out in the evening haze.
The heath's aroma, spreads far and wide
Of thyme and solitude
From afar impends the town smells,
While from the hills, the sea pales.

Seeräuber

Wilde Sage, blaue Sage
Von den Ahnen, den Uskoken
In den weissen Küstenstädten
Hatten steil sie ihre Nester
Auf den Engen, auf den Inseln,
In dem Rauberturm von Ljubač.
Sassen auf den Vorgebirgen
Augen auf den Venezianer,
Spanten übers Meer wie Fänge
Ihre schnellen Segel aus

Wenn die Bora von den Bergen
Niedersprang so blau und selig,
O wie glogen ihre Schiffe
O wie flatterte ihr Haar!
Salzig schmeckten ihre Lippen,
Wurzig roch es von den Inseln
Und die braunen Hände packten
Reiche Levantinerfracht.

Sea Raiders

Wild legends, blue legends
Of the *Uskok* forefathers
In the white coastal towns
On the crags they keep their nests,
In the isthmus, on the islands
Stood the raider tower Ljubač
There they stood on the foothills
Scouting for the Venetians
Hoisting their sails briskly
As if casting their nets widely to sea

When the Bora plunged down
From the mountains, so blue and blessed
Oh, how her ships were flying,
Oh, how her hair was flapping
Salty tasted her lips
Full flavour from the islands
And the brown hands snatched
Bountiful Levantine freight

Guter Kaiser, ferner Kaiser
Um das wilde Volk zu zähmen,
Häuser gab er, Weizenäcker
Heimatsrecht im grünen Land
Siedelte die braunen Brüder
An die sanften zahmen Tälern,

Dass sie hausten, dass sie säten,
Fromm nach alter Bauerart.
Doch die wilden Räubersöhne
Wollten nicht im Tale wohnen,
Wollten nicht den Weizen bauen,
Hassten Dorf und grünes Land.
Von den Häusern und den Äckern
Nieder an die blaue Küste
Wieder wie von Berg die Bora
Stürzte die Uskokenschar

Good Kaiser, far Kaiser
To tame the wild people
He gave houses, fields of wheat
A new home in the green land.
Where settled the browned brothers
In smooth, tame valleys

So that they dwelled, So that they sowed
Piously in the old peasant way
Yet the wild raiders sons
Defied to dwell in the valley,
Refused to grow the wheat,
Despised the village and the green land.
Away from the houses and fields
Once more, down the blue coast
Like the Bora from the mountain,
Plunged the *Uskok* hordes.

Wieder durch die Inselengen
Jagten sie die Venezianer
Hatten Salz auf ihren Lippen
Und es flog ihr Haar im Wind
Bargen sich in dunklen Buchten
Bei dem Nachtgeschrei der Möwen
Häuften wieder bunte Schätze
In dem alten Räuberturm

Wilde Seele, meine Seele,
Tochter bist du der Piraten,
Tochter du der blauen Bora,
Tochter du des Inselmeers
Kannst nicht lang in Tale wohnen,
Wie die Ahnen, die Uskoken,
Sehnsucht treibt dich immer wieder
Nieder wie vom Berg die Bora
Nieder an die blaue Küste
An der Heimat wildes Herz

Once more through the island's straits
Hounded they the Venetians
Had salt on their lips
And their hair flew in the wind
Harbored in dark bays
At the night jowl of the gulls
Again, heaping up the colorful treasure
In the old raiders tower

Wild soul, my soul
You are daughter of the pirates
Daughter of the blue Bora
Daughter of the sea of islands,
Cannot bear long living in the valley
Like the Uskok forefathers,
Longing compels you time and again
Down from the mountain like the Bora,
Down to the blue shore,
To the homeland's wild heart.

MAP OF DALMATIA
IN THE AUSTRIAN EMPIRE

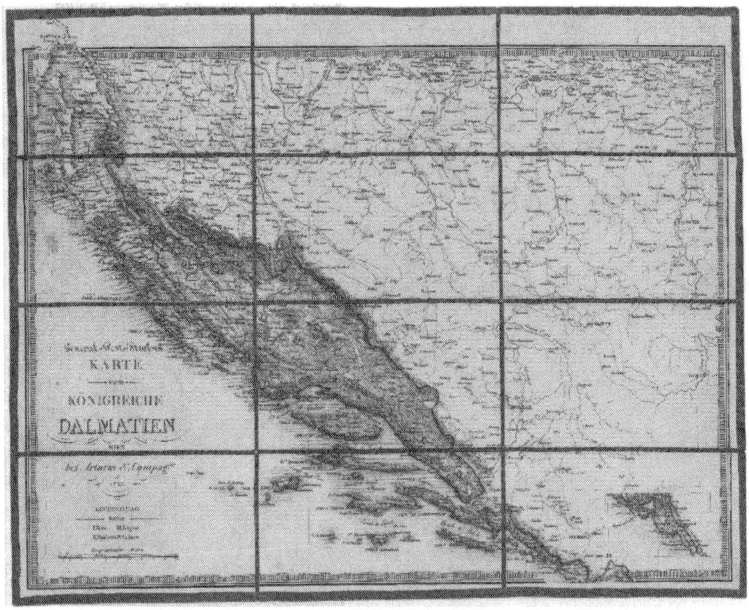

ZADAR ARCHIVE, CROATIA, WITH PERMISSION

BIBLIOGRAPHY OF
PAULA VON PRERADOVIĆ'S WORK

Poetry

Dalmatinische Sonette, 1933
Lob Gottes im Gebirge, 1936
Ritter, Tod und Teufel, 1946

Prose

Pave und Pero, 1940
Königslegende, 1950
Die Versuchung des Columba, 1951
Wiener Chronik, 1945

TRANSLATOR BIOGRAPHIES

Irina Pavlović is a research associate at the Slavic Institute of the University of Hamburg and has been a teacher of English, German, and Russian at secondary schools in Hamburg and Bremen. Previously, she worked as a research assistant in the Department of English at the University of Bremen and was the Nick Müller fellow at the University of New Orleans in 2018/2019.

Of Croatian and Serbian lineage, she ultimately sees herself as Tyrolean above all.

Vicko Marelić is a historian and museum curator in the town museum on the island of Korčula, Croatia. Although born and raised in Great Britain, most of his summers were spent on the pictoresque Dalmatian island where he now works. After studies in England and France, he decided to follow the trail of the Habsburg myth and ended up living the European dream in Vienna, where he worked as an English teacher in a secondary school for several years. Starting a PhD in history at the University of Vienna that focused on the British diplomatic history regarding Adriatic, he gained several fellowships such as a stint at the Austrian historical institute in Rome. Thanks to the generosity of the Austrian Ministry of Sciences, he was a fellow at the university of New Orleans in 2018-2019. This translation project took off on the other side of the Atlantic, as a tribute to the Alpine-Adriatic realms that have captured his imagination.